THE LITTLE BOOK OF

Restorative Discipline for Schools

THE LITTLE BOOKS OF JUSTICE & PEACEBUILDING

Published titles include:

The Little Book of Restorative Justice, by Howard Zehr

El Pequeño Libro De Justicia Restaurativa, by Howard Zehr

The Little Book of Conflict Transformation, by John Paul Lederach

The Little Book of Family Group Conferences, New-Zealand Style,
by Allan MacRae and Howard Zehr

The Little Book of Strategic Peacebuilding, by Lisa Schirch

The Little Book of Strategic Negotiation,
by Jayne Seminare Docherty

The Little Book of Circle Processes, by Kay Pranis

The Little Book of Contemplative Photography, by Howard Zehr

The Little Book of Restorative Discipline for Schools,
by Lorraine Stutzman Amstutz and Judy H. Mullet

The Little Book of Trauma Healing, by Carolyn Yoder

The Little Book of Biblical Justice, by Chris Marshall

The Little Book of Restorative Justice for People in Prison,
by Barb Toews

The Little Book of Cool Tools for Hot Topics,
by Ron Kraybill and Evelyn Wright

The Little Book of Dialogue for Difficult Subjects,
by Lisa Schirch and David Campt

The Little Book of Victim Offender Conferencing,
by Lorraine Stutzman Amstutz

The Little Book of Healthy Organizations,
by David R. Brubaker and Ruth Hoover Zimmerman

The Little Books of Justice & Peacebuilding present, in highly accessible form, key concepts and practices from the fields of restorative justice, conflict transformation, and peacebuilding. Written by leaders in these fields, they are designed for practitioners, students, and anyone interested in justice, peace, and conflict resolution.

The Little Books of Justice & Peacebuilding series is a cooperative effort between the Center for Justice and Peacebuilding of Eastern Mennonite University (Howard Zehr, Series General Editor) and publisher Good Books (Phyllis Pellman Good, Senior Editor).

THE LITTLE BOOK OF
Restorative Discipline for Schools

Teaching responsibility; creating caring climates

LORRAINE STUTZMAN AMSTUTZ
AND JUDY H. MULLET

Good Books

Intercourse, PA 17534
800/762-7171
www.GoodBooks.com

Acknowledgments

From Lorraine: A special heartfelt thanks to my spouse, Jim, who continually encourages me to be all that I can be and supports me on that journey. Thanks also to my children, Solomon, Jordan, and Leah, who courageously allow me to practice what I preach.

From Judy: To my mother who taught me to be an artist for peace no matter what my occupation. To my father who taught me not to criticize an idea unless I had a more life-giving thought to offer. To my children and spouse who bring me tenderness.

Both of us would like to thank those who provided inspiration, suggestions, and critical review of this *Little Book*, with special thanks to Howard Zehr for his constant encouragement.

Cover photograph by Howard Zehr.

Design by Dawn J. Ranck

THE LITTLE BOOK OF RESTORATIVE DISCIPLINE FOR SCHOOLS
Copyright © 2005 by Good Books, Intercourse, PA 17534
International Standard Book Number: 1-56148-506-3
Library of Congress Catalog Card Number: 2005018011

Library of Congress Cataloging-in-Publication Data

Amstutz, Lorraine Stutzman.
The little book of restorative discipline for schools : teaching responsibility, creating caring climates / Lorraine Stutzman Amstutz and Judy H. Mullet.
p. cm.
Includes bibliographical references.
ISBN 1-56148-506-3 (pbk.)
1. School discipline. 2. Conflict management. 3. Restorative justice. 4. Teacher-student relationships. I. Mullet, Judy H. II. Title.
LB3012.A52 2005
371.5--dc22   2005018011

Table of Contents

1.
Introduction

The secret of education lies in respecting the pupil.

— Ralph Waldo Emerson

Situations requiring discipline in our schools can, in fact, be opportunities for learning, growth, and community-building. This idea is based on the assumption put forth by Nel Noddings, author of *Caring: A Feminine Approach to Ethics and Moral Education,* that "the aim of education is to reveal an attainable image of self that is lovelier than that manifested in his or her present acts."[1]

For this to happen, we will need to move beyond viewing discipline as punishment, or even as problem-solving, to a more holistic perspective that sees all aspects of behavior as related. A number of developments in education and related fields are already pointing in this direction. We will especially draw upon two of these.

First, the "peaceable school" concept acknowledges that education is *for* and *by* the community. This concept has been widely recognized and written about within education and has significant implications for our subject. Second, the principles and values of restorative justice have much to say about the way we live in community with one another, including in our schools. Although in our Western culture, restorative justice emerged initially within the criminal justice field, this approach is increasingly gaining recognition and application in the educational arena.

This book draws upon these and other concepts and provides some suggestions about how a restorative approach might be applied to discipline and problem-solving in schools. However, we don't propose a cookie-cutter approach to restorative discipline; to imply such would oversimplify complex and diverse community situations. Rather, a restorative approach is a philosophy or framework that can guide us as we design programs and make decisions within our particular settings.

> Restorative discipline is a philosophy or framework.

We urge you to think about the values and principles of restorative justice and to adapt them to fit your situation. We believe that doing so honors the strength and competencies within your own setting.

We offer this *Little Book* as a resource for teachers and administrators. We hope it can be a helpful addition to the knowledge and expertise already available to you within your school.

We begin by telling two stories that for some may sound too good to be true, too pie-in-the-sky. We tell these stories, however, to show the potential we believe a restorative approach has for our schools, recognizing that much of what we talk about is like planting seeds.

We have no illusions that implementing restorative approaches is the "cure" for all behavior issues. We also have stories of frustration, of working with students in situations where it seemed uncertain whether the seeds would take root. But the following two stories demonstrate that encouraging empathy can foster compassion and motivate right choices. When we ask our children to put themselves in others' shoes, possibilities can become reality.

Someone once noted that there are at least 500 choices in every conflict situation. Options not yet considered exist daily in our classrooms. To discover these options requires creative thinking and a sense of possibility. We believe this vision of untried possibilities is the new but often neglected frontier in community education. We hope these stories will help foster this vision in your educational setting.

The turkey prank[2]

What do you get when you put five graduating seniors, five or six turkeys, and a need to be remembered, together in an empty high school late at night? Answer: A disaster.

The original plan was to take the turkeys from a local turkey farm, put them in the high school to run around all night, and make a mess. However, once inside the school, the young men reported that everyone's adrenaline kicked in and a crowd mentality took over.

Turkeys were stuffed into lockers so they would fly out at unsuspecting students the next morning. One turkey was butchered and bled up and down the halls before dying. Another turkey was so disoriented it ran into a floor-to-ceiling window and broke its neck. The mayhem was indescribable when the janitor arrived for school the next day. The job before him seemed horrific.

The case went through the legal system, but the judge realized the small community had gaping wounds that the legal system could not address. So the case was referred to the local restorative justice program for a conference.

When the case was received by the program, a decision needed to be made about whom to invite to the conference in addition to the five young men and their parents, who had already agreed to attend. Individuals, including a member of the faith community, were chosen to represent the community at large. The superintendent, principal, three school-board members, three teachers, and the janitor were asked to participate. A member of the media was asked to join the conference, with the understanding that he was there as a community member. The total number of attendees was 35, which included one lead facilitator and five trained community volunteer facilitators.

The process of pre-conferencing with participants began with a meeting of the five seniors and their parents. A second meeting was held with representatives of the school community, and it included the visibly angry janitor. The janitor wanted to participate but insisted he would not be part of a conference in which they would get him to "sing Kum Ba Yah."

The tension during the final conference was high as it began. School representatives spoke first about their feelings of anger and betrayal, while at the same time acknowledging the students' positive qualities.

The students were also given an opportunity to speak and talked of how the prank escalated out of control. They expressed shame and embarrassment because of their behavior and apologized to those present, including their parents. The final young man to speak was flushed and shaking. He commented about how difficult it was for him to walk down Main Street and make eye contact with anyone because he was so ashamed of what he had done.

Near the end of the conference, the facilitator asked if there were final comments. The janitor raised his hand and the room fell silent. He addressed all of the young men, saying he accepted their apologies. He then turned to the last young man who had spoken and said to him, "The next time you see me on the street, you can look me in the eye because I will remember you for who you were tonight and not for what you did."

An environment of care[3]

I visited an elementary peaceable school on the same day that school learned it had won a statewide award for excellence in education. The principal led me and my group of prospective teachers on a jubilant tour of the school. The school's educators had designed the building. They insisted on changes that made the architects groan, but which they believed would foster the kind of community they envisioned. Parents of first-graders chose their individual student's classroom, and, thus, which method of reading instruction they wanted for their child. Parents only were hired as assistants in the classroom, and community volunteers were visible throughout the building.

In the middle of the school was a cultural center honoring community traditions. In the media center, all materials were accessible to both teachers and students. The school enjoyed long lists of teachers who wanted to work there.

The principal was quick to note that the school received no more monies than any other school in the district. When I asked him what discipline system they had developed, he paused for a moment, then mused, "I guess we don't have one. We just don't have discipline problems." I had visited scores of schools in four states during my tenure as a school psychologist and college professor, but never one with an ethos of peace and community engagement like this one.

Then I visited another school on this same tour. Down the road a mile or so was a high school that the children in the school I just described would eventually attend. As I entered I noticed huge holes in the tiles on the floor. I learned that the lockers were recently moved to a place where adults could view them all of the time because students had set fires in them in their old location. When the bell rang at the start of each period, the teachers would lock the classroom doors to keep out mischievous students. Three rooms were reserved for in-school suspension. Teacher turnover was high, and an air of suspicion and fear permeated the school. What happened on the road between the two schools? How was caring unlearned?

2.
Why Restorative Discipline?

The role of discipline

One of the greatest concerns of parents and educators is how to assist our children, through teaching and guidance, to become responsible and caring adults. Providing adequate and appropriate discipline is an important part of this proces.

The term *discipline* comes from an old English word and means "to teach or train." Discipline is teaching children rules to live by and helping them become socialized into their culture. That socialization is a lifelong process and includes helping children to control their impulses and to develop social skills that allow them to fully participate in lifelong interactions with others around them.

Discipline usually has several goals. Short-term, discipline intends to stop a child's inappropriate behavior while explaining what is appropriate. Long-term, discipline aims to help them take responsibility for their own behavior. When children's lives and behavior are too regulated by others, they feel no need to control themselves since others do it for them. So an important long-term goal is to teach self-discipline.

Restorative discipline adds to the current discipline models, which attempt to prevent or stop misbehavior, and teaches more life-giving responses. In today's schools, care for the person(s) harmed through misbehavior is rarely addressed in intentional ways. Restorative discipline helps misbehaving students deal with the harm they have caused to individuals and to the school community. The goals of restorative discipline apply not only to those involved in or affected by misbehavior, but to the larger educational community as well.

Key goals of restorative discipline

- To understand the harm and develop empathy for both the harmed and the harmer.

- To listen and respond to the needs of the person harmed and the person who harmed.

- To encourage accountability and responsibility through personal reflection within a collaborative planning process.

- To reintegrate the harmer (and, if necessary, the harmed) into the community as valuable, contributing members.

- To create caring climates to support healthy communities.

- To change the system when it contributes to the harm.

Discipline, then, becomes a long-term process that hopefully leads our children to become responsible for their own behavior. Teaching self-discipline requires time, patience, and respect for our children. We need to invest the required time it takes in order to prepare our children for life.

How do we do that in the context of school life? We know that children misbehave and that they do so for a variety of reasons. They may still be learning the difference between right and wrong. They may be upset, discouraged, or feeling rejected. They may be feeling powerless in a particular situation. Or they simply may be acting their age; misbehavior is often associated with particular developmental stages of life.

But even though children may follow similar overall patterns of development from one stage to another, they do not all reach and leave each stage at the same time. Each child has his or her own internal developmental timetable, so each progresses uniquely. This becomes a source of unpredictability for parents and teachers and gives rise to a feeling that we can never figure them out.

> Discipline is a long-term process that leads children to become responsible.

We do know that differentiated instruction is successful when teachers plan for different learning rates and styles and when they structure tasks to meet individual needs. We believe that discipline should be equally individualized to meet the needs of students; we will discuss that more fully in a later chapter.

The role of punishment

Nelsen, Lott, and Glenn, in their book *Positive Discipline in the Classroom*, ask, "Where did we ever get the crazy idea that to make people do better we first have to make them feel worse?"[4] In general, punishment serves to restrain a child temporarily but does little to teach self-discipline directly. Punishment may make children obey the rules when the enforcer is present or nearby, and it may teach them to comply in the short run. But does it teach the skills needed to understand the meaning behind the rules?

The negative effects of punishment are well documented.[5] These include feelings of anger by the one being punished which change the focus from the harm done to resenting the giver of the painful punishment. The punished student then tends to question the nature of the punishment and to blame the punisher rather than take responsibility for the harm done by the misbehavior. Punished students exhibit a domino effect: they blame teachers, take out their frustration on peers, and passively resist assigned work.

Punishment often has negative side effects and does little to teach self-discipline.

So why does punishment continue to be the dominant feature in school discipline? The most obvious answer is that it is quick, easy to administer, and seems to meet the criterion that "at least something was done." Teachers often feel frustrated when they send students to the office because of misbehavior, only to have the students sent back after a conversation with the administrator. This often does not seem like an adequate response. Many students are not willing to face the harm they have done, nor to take responsibility for their behavior. When this happens, punishment may seem necessary to restrict opportunities for more harm.

There may be a place for some forms of punishment in these situations. A punishment-as-transition focus would allow punishment but continue to offer opportunities for choosing more positive options. For some students, punishment is best viewed as beginning the discipline process of moving toward healthier decision-making and responsible behavior. A specific plan and action for responsible change should follow and replace the punishment measure. Support for such change will come from those affected by the misbehavior, including friends and relatives of the person who caused harm.

Restorative discipline, like punishment, concerns itself with appropriate consequences that encourage accountability—but accountability that emphasizes empathy and repair of harm. Restorative practices also encourage accountability through a collaborative, community-owned process. Ideally, we could design processes that use punishment, or the threat of punishment, as a *last* resort, with restorative options as the norm or default. This is what New Zealand has done, for example, in their youth justice system where the first response is a restorative conference, and the use of court and punishment is reserved for those situations that cannot be successfully resolved through a restorative process.[6]

The role of restorative justice

The concept of restorative justice has been articulated during the past 30 years, at least for those of us with a Western worldview, as a way to address some of the problems and limitations of the Western legal system. Victims, offenders, and communities often feel that the legal system has not met their needs for justice. Those within the system, too, often felt frustrated at the system's failure to provide genuine accountability for offenders and to address the needs of those who have been harmed.

The restorative justice field has introduced a number of ways to address these issues in practice through various forms of mediation, conferencing and circles, many of which have application in restorative discipline. However, restorative justice has also offered a different perspective or philosophy from which to view wrongdoing. This perspective focuses on needs and resulting obligations more than on making sure people get what they "deserve." It also emphasizes collaborative and cooperative problem-solving.

Restorative justice emphasizes needs and resulting obligations more than "deserts."

In *The Little Book of Restorative Justice,* Howard Zehr notes that our understanding of how to handle wrongdoing often revolves around three questions: What rules were broken? Who did it? What do they deserve?[7] This tends to leave those who were harmed out of the process, focusing instead on the punishment of those who offended. As we have seen above, punishment is often ineffective or counter-productive.

A restorative approach, Zehr reasons, centers around six guiding questions.

Guiding questions for a restorative approach

1. Who has been hurt?

2. What are their needs?

3. Whose obligations are they?

4. What are the causes?

5. Who has a "stake" in this?

6. What is the appropriate process to involve stakeholders in an effort to put things right?

Zehr proposes a definition for restorative justice designed for a criminal justice setting:

Why Restorative Discipline?

Restorative justice is a process to involve, to the extent possible, those who have a stake in a specific offense and to collectively identify and address harms, needs, and obligations, in order to heal and put things as right as possible.

Many have begun to look at the principles and practices of restorative justice to address issues in other arenas beyond the legal justice system. For example, how do we deal with issues of harm and wrongdoing *before* they reach the legal system? How do we teach our children about accountability and responsibility? What lessons do children learn about how to deal with conflict and with difficult situations in which they find themselves? What about the interpersonal conflicts students bring to school that originate outside school hours? Restorative justice promotes values and principles that encourage us to listen and speak to one another in ways that validate the experiences and needs of everyone within the community.

We would like to propose a broader definition that addresses not only the responsive nature of restorative justice when a harm or violation occurs, but provides a guide to how we live together day by day:

Restorative justice promotes values and principles that use inclusive, collaborative approaches for being in community. These approaches validate the experiences and needs of everyone within the community, particularly those who have been marginalized, oppressed, or harmed. These approaches allow us to act and respond in ways that are healing rather than alienating or coercive.

This definition of restorative justice or discipline has implications for problem-solving and discipline in a school setting. Let's explore this further with two scenarios:

Scenario A: A teacher walks into his eighth-grade homeroom class early one morning and hears Jason call Sam an inappropriate name. He takes Jason into the hallway and talks to him about his language and how that must make Sam feel. He lets him know that kind of language will not be tolerated and the behavior must stop. Jason begins to tell him what happened, but the teacher reiterates his position that the language Jason used was wrong and must not happen again.

They go back into the classroom and the teacher pulls both Jason and Sam aside and tells them he notices they are treating each other unkindly and wants that behavior to stop—from both of them. Class resumes. Sam and Jason continue to be angry at each other.

Scenario B: A teacher walks into his homeroom class early one morning and hears Jason call Sam an inappropriate name. He asks both Sam and Jason to come out into the hallway and tells them he would like to meet with them together immediately following lunch back in their classroom.

During that meeting he asks Sam and Jason what has been going on between them that seems to be causing such difficulties over the past two weeks. Jason talks about Sam taking his assignment book during homeroom and hiding it. Jason knows that Sam was joking, but when he kept doing it, Jason became irritated and asked Sam to stop. Sam continued with the prank, and Jason got in trouble yesterday because his English homework was in the book, and he could not find where Sam had hidden it. Jason felt frustrated and called Sam a name, which is what the teacher heard that morning.

Sam acknowledged that perhaps he had gotten carried away with his joking and did not know Jason had gotten into trouble. And Sam told Jason he didn't think his actions warranted the name that Jason called him in front of everyone. Both boys apologized and agreed that things had gotten out of control and that they didn't want the trouble to continue.

Scenario B is the response most likely to bring about long-term positive results within the school environment, even though it obviously takes more time. We believe that restorative justice provides one framework to reach that goal.

Restorative discipline in schools is not simply about introducing new programs and/or practices, although that is a key component. It is also about providing a new *framework* for the work that educators are doing. Certainly teachers can utilize ad hoc restorative discipline practices alongside existing school policies. The ideal, however, is to have schools—including parents and students—look at existing policies and practices and discern together how to replace those practices that have not worked and implement restorative discipline approaches for the entire school or system.

As parents we recall times when we have regretted decisions we made regarding the discipline of our children. Looking back on some of those decisions we recognize one key missing factor: creativity. That lack of creativity led to discipline that was more about our need for control or quick resolution rather than about our children's lifelong learning. When dealing with a conflict we often do not view it as an opportunity or a teachable moment but, rather, something to get through.

We know that teachers, administrators, parents, practitioners, and others working in educational settings already have disciplinary toolboxes. Our hope is that restorative discipline approaches will provide an additional toolbox, one that holds many new resources yet to be discovered.

> If you want to solve a problem, you cannot solve it if you continue to think the same way you were thinking when you created it.
>
> — Albert Einstein

Restorative discipline approaches can provide new and creative possibilities rather than simply offering cookie-cutter answers to situations which teachers and administrators experience every day. Restorative discipline requires flexibility and creativity. It requires thinking about the behaviors that rules are meant to regulate, more than the rules themselves, and being aware of the unintended consequences of rules. It means giving attention to how we learn to live and work together.

Other roots of restorative discipline

We have noted the contribution of the restorative justice field to restorative discipline. A number of other movements and perspectives have also contributed significantly.

A primary goal of schools in a democracy is to develop a community of responsible citizens. In recent years, three movements in education—Conflict Resolution Education, Character Education, and Emotional Literacy—have broadened the focus of democratic schools.

Conflict Resolution Education (CRE) introduced peer mediation programs and developed curricula to integrate conflict resolution into school life. What began as instruction in nonviolent problem-solving developed into a peaceable schools approach that honors an ethos of care within collaborative communities.

CRE most directly influenced discipline in schools through peer mediation programs, which often served as an alternative or add-on to existing discipline processes dictated by adults. When students assisted each other in developing ways to manage and change behavior, the question naturally arose: Why can't all students learn the skills to mange their own conflicts? CRE now teaches negotiation as well as mediation skills to students, in addition to those who receive specific training as mediators.

The Character Education (CE) movement developed separately but informed the relationship-building element, or peaceable schools component, of CRE. Character Education programs are primarily designed to teach and encourage positive values and behavior. Therefore, they do not focus heavily on the specific options in conflict situations or on how such situations can transform behavior.

However, CE programs have developed materials to teach such core values as responsibility, respect, trustworthiness, and friendship, as well as how to care for oneself, for others, for the environment, and for ideas. All of these values are important to a restorative perspective.

Daniel Goleman's work in *Emotional Literacy* provided impetus for schools to attend to both the affective and cognitive components crucial to learning in a diverse society.[8] Each of these three movements has contributed to the emergence of restorative discipline.

Building on the lessons of these three other movements, restorative discipline intentionally focuses on the relational and transformative elements of discipline, both in the processes of working through the conflicts, and in the product or outcome of these processes.

> Restorative discipline prefers collaborative solutions.

While the primary question CRE asks is, "How can you solve the problem?", in restorative discipline the key question is, "How can you put it right?". The first focuses on finding a solution that is fair and acceptable to all parties; restorative discipline adds the additional layer of working on the relationship that was harmed or deterred. It also seeks to include all those affected by the action in a collaborative process of developing a plan for change and restitution.

In addition to these contributing movements, three major philosophical strands have shaped restorative discipline most extensively: constructivism, critical reflection, and psycho-educational theory.

Constructivism holds that individuals gain meaning and motivation when they are given power to make their own decisions and to engage in the problem-solving process through collaboration.

Critical reflection describes a problem-solving process that honors multiple perspectives and emphasizes creative problem-solving along with an analysis of systems and situations.

A *psycho-education* approach values an understanding of the internal feelings, needs, and conflicts that motivate behavior. As we have seen, restorative justice theory has added a focus on the relationship piece: the harm done by misbehavior and the consequent need to put things as right as possible. We will explore restorative principles and values further in Chapter 3.

A punishment-to-restoration continuum

Restorative discipline does not seek to deny consequences for misbehavior. Instead, it focuses on helping students understand the real harm done by their misbehavior, to take responsibility for the behavior, and to commit to positive change. We propose a continuum of discipline measures or choices in education, moving from *punishment* to *consequences* to *solutions* to *restoration*.

A discipline continuum

Punishment   *Consequences*   *Solutions*   *Restoration*

◄───►

Within the *punishment approach*, consequences are selected without any meaningful connection between the misbehavior and the punishment; e.g., suspension for stealing sneakers and trashing the locker room. A *consequences approach* seeks to make the punishment fit the crime by linking natural or artificially connected consequences to the crime. This may mean that the student's consequence is to clean the locker room. These consequences are selected by adults or a peer jury based on a menu of options that are seen as connected to the misbehavior; e.g., the student "corrects" the harm done.

A *solutions approach* sees misbehavior as a problem to be solved. In the case above, the disciplinary procedure would look at why the student was in the locker room and was motivated to vandalize it and steal sneakers. Educators are familiar with a "functional behavior assessment" approach.

It seeks to find the function or purpose of the misbehavior, and then to develop a plan to replace the misbehavior with a positive behavior which meets the needs of the student but without breaking rules. In the stealing example, a disciplinarian might find, after interviewing observers, that the student who stole the shoes was upset because the owner of the shoes was getting more playing time than he was. The plan for change might include a new way to address play-time concerns.

When using punishment, consequences, and solution modes, adults typically select the plan or consequence without the input of the misbehaving student. Some form of retribution is usually meted out in this process, even if solutions are chosen to address an underlying issue. A *restorative approach*, however, recognizes the needs and purposes behind the misbehavior, as well as the needs of those who were harmed by the misbehavior. A restorative approach works with all participants to create ways to put things right and make plans for future change. Thus, the focus is on the healing that can occur through a collaborative conferencing process.

Restorative discipline:

- recognizes the purposes of misbehavior

- addresses the needs of those harmed

- works to put right the harm

- aims to improve the future

- seeks to heal

- uses collaborative processes

Why Restorative Discipline?

Both punishment and consequence modes are based on the hope that unpleasant results or pain will deter misbehavior. The solutions mode holds that solving the presenting problem will deter future misbehavior and provide a more healthy replacement behavior. The restorative discipline mode believes that harmers will choose respectful options when they come to understand, through dialogue and conversation with those harmed, the pain they have caused by their misbehavior. The following story illustrates an approach to misbehavior that initially was punitive but became restorative.

A solutions approach holds that solving problems will encourage healthier behavior.

Amy, a 13-year-old, was told "No!" by her mother when she asked to attend a particular event with friends. Amy responded with anger, slamming doors and being disrespectful, especially after her mother's reason for saying No amounted to "Because I said so." This continued throughout the afternoon until the mother reacted by imposing consequences. Amy was grounded for a three-week period.

A high level of anxiety and tension continued until the two of them sat down to discuss what had happened, acknowledging their mutual anger which resulted in what seemed to Amy to be an unfair punishment. Amy said the exchange taught her that she shouldn't be angry because she would be punished. Her mother responded that the punishment was a result of *how* Amy inappropriately displayed her anger, rather than the anger itself.

> As they continued to talk Amy agreed that her behavior required consequences. She wondered whether there were options other than being grounded and suggested that she cook the family meals for one week in exchange for one week of grounding.

Ideally, the conversation about Amy's inappropriate anger would have happened before the punishment, but the level of intensity was obviously high and the level of creativity low. Allowing Amy to have a say in the consequences of her actions provided a number of opportunities beyond simply grounding her for three weeks.

The new solution gave Amy and her mother and/or father an opportunity to spend time together for a week while cooking the family meals. This taught Amy valuable life skills and provided additional time for her parents to talk about the reasons Amy was not allowed to attend the event with her friends. It gave them an opportunity to have the kind of discussion that is often difficult in the midst of a conflict. They were able to talk about their relationship rather than simply the presenting issue. And it provided an opportunity to look at the underlying feelings of hurt both might have been feeling. They could then begin to talk about the values that are important in creating meaningful relationships.

Let us turn, now, to the values and principles that underlie and shape restorative discipline.

3.
Values and Principles of Restorative Discipline

Many schools have already developed value statements which they use in their policies and their code of ethics. These values are intended to set expectations for all involved in the school community. Many of these values already reflect the broader values of restorative justice. They may include respect, truthfulness, dependability, self-control, self-discipline, acceptance, responsibility, and accountability.

Restorative justice emphasizes many of these values and articulates principles based on these values. In his *Little Book of Restorative Justice,* Zehr spells out the basic principles of restorative justice:

Restorative justice . . .

1. Focuses on *harms* and consequent needs (the victims', as well as the communities' and the offenders').

2. Addresses *obligations* resulting from those harms (the offenders', but also the communities' and the society's).

3. Uses *inclusive, collaborative* processes.

4. *Involves* those with a legitimate *stake* in the situation (victims, offenders, community members, society).

5. Seeks to *put right* the wrongs.

All of these principles must be rooted in respect for others. Below are a number of principles reflecting values and concepts for implementing restorative discipline in school settings. Under each principle are some of its important implications. We have been inspired by, and have adapted the work of, many others.

Restorative discipline . . .

1. Acknowledges that relationships are central to building community.
   • Restorative discipline seeks to strengthen relationships and build community by encouraging a caring school climate.
   • Every student, teacher, administrator, and staff member is a valued member of the school community.
   • Students should be involved in a process of naming the values and principles to live by within their school community.
   • Extra-curricular activities are best structured when they build ties between students and ties to the community.

2. Builds *systems* that address misbehavior and harm in a way that strengthens relationships.
   • Schools establish policies to provide a safe place for learning. Real safety, however, comes from fostering and maintaining caring relationships.

- Policies should reflect the values and principles agreed to by the school community.
- Policies need to address the root causes of discipline problems rather than only the symptoms. The causes of misbehavior may be multiple and each should be addressed.
- It is best to structure a school as a series of small units, eg., in order to make it easier to build community through relationships.

3. Focuses on the harm done rather than only on rule-breaking.
   - Misbehavior is an offense against people and relationships, not just rule-breaking.
   - The solution to the offense needs to involve all of those harmed by the misbehavior.
   - The person harmed is the center of the primary relationship that needs to be addressed. Secondary relationships that may have been impacted might include other students, teachers, parents, the administration, and the surrounding community.
   - Much misbehavior arises out of attempts to address a perceived injustice. Those who are victimized also feel they have been treated unjustly. Discipline processes must leave room for addressing these perceptions.

4. Gives voice to the person harmed.
   - The immediate safety concerns of the person harmed are primary.
   - Those harmed must be given an opportunity to have a voice in the resolution of the harm.

5. Engages in collaborative problem-solving.
   - Misbehavior creates both danger and opportunities for those involved.

- All of us act to satisfy our human needs (for belonging, freedom, power, and fun). Students choose behaviors to meet these underlying needs.
- Family, students, and communities are encouraged to help identify problems and solutions that meet needs.
- Misbehavior can become a teachable moment if everyone is involved.

6. Empowers change and growth.
   - In order for students to change and grow, we must help them identify their needs and assist them in finding alternative, life giving ways of meeting those needs.
   - Interpersonal conflict is a part of living in relationship with others.
   - Conflict presents opportunity for change if the process includes careful listening, reflecting, shared problem-solving, trust, and accountability structures that support commitments to work at relationship-building.

7. Enhances Responsibility.
   - Real responsibility requires one to understand the impact of her or his actions on others, along with an attempt to acknowledge and put things right when that impact is negative.
   - Consequences should be evaluated based on whether they are reasonable, related to the offense, restorative, and respectful.
   - Students should continually be invited to become responsible and cooperative.
   - Some students choose to resist change and need adults to make decisions concerning their accountability.
   - At times, persisting in "walking behind" (to let the student know someone is there if needed) rather than

"walking alongside" (to monitor or cue the student regarding appropriate behavior) is necessary before a student is ready to acknowledge the harm of a behavior.

Before implementing any approaches, we suggest that you test your ideas against the following restorative discipline yardstick that reflects the principles above.

A restorative discipline yardstick

You are working toward restorative discipline in schools when you . . .

1. Focus primarily on relationships and secondarily on rules.
   - Does the proposed response go beyond focusing solely on policy violations? Is equal concern also being given to harms experienced by individuals and the community?
   - What steps are being implemented to ensure the safety of the individuals involved while information is being gathered?
   - Have support people (e.g., an advocate, pastor, mentor, or other person deemed appropriate given the circumstances) been identified, approved by, and provided for each person involved?
   - Are needed resources available for all persons involved, i.e., transportation, childcare, an interpreter, accessibility?
   - Has the issue of whether or not to maintain confidentiality within the process and the findings been addressed?
   - Are there mandated reporting issues?

- How will information be shared more broadly if necessary?

2. Give voice to the person(s) harmed.
   - Does the response address the needs of the person harmed, both the immediate victim as well as others who may be affected? Does it allow an opportunity for those harmed to be part of the resolution? Has the person harmed been asked what s/he needs? Has the person harmed been asked what a just process would look like?

3. Give voice to person(s) who caused the harm.
   - Has the person who harmed been asked what s/he needs?
   - Does the response address the needs of the person who did the harm?
   - Does it allow an opportunity for those who harmed to be part of the resolution?
   - Has the person who harmed been asked what s/he can give/offer?
   - Has the person who harmed been asked what a just process would look like?

4. Engage in collaborative problem-solving.
   - Are the solutions being arrived at collaboratively, meaning that all those affected (or representatives of those affected) by the harm/incident are fully involved? Are all participants represented at the decision-making table? Are all decisions reached collaboratively, with assurance that all voices are heard?
   - Given the imbalances that often exist between persons and institutions, have these been recognized, acknowledged, discussed, and addressed?

5. Enhance Responsibility.
   * Does the response help the person take responsibility for the harm caused, or does it focus primarily on punishment?
   * Does the person who caused the harm understand how his/her actions have affected other people? If not, is there a plan in place that includes steps to assist the person in a process of understanding (which may include education on a particular issue, counseling, or training)?
   * Is there an acknowledgement that some persons choose to resist change and need others to assist in making decisions regarding their accountability? The consequences in that case may need to be made or suggested by others involved in decision-making.

6. Empower Change and Growth.
   * Does the response allow the person who harmed to be involved in the process of repair with a concern toward that individual's growth and competency?
   * Has the individual acknowledged responsibility for the harm of his/her actions? If not, what steps should be taken to address ways of meeting and supporting that person's need for growth and competency?

7. Plan for Restoration.
   * Does the response allow for the person who harmed, as well as the person harmed, to be supported and reintegrated back into the community?
   * Has the issue of accountability been appropriately addressed to the satisfaction of the person harmed?
   * Has a process been developed that ensures ongoing accountability if an agreement for next steps is reached?

- Is there recognition that one possible solution is a "parting of ways" (or setting procedures to avoid interaction), in an effort to give primary consideration to the needs of the person harmed?

In Chapter 5 we will look at various models and applications of these principles. However, restorative discipline is not just about addressing individual situations or problems. It is also about the importance of creating an overall environment that discourages wrongdoing and fosters restorative responses. This is the subject of Chapter 4.

4.
Toward a Restorative Environment

The peaceable schools component of restorative discipline is the preventive and instructional arm of a restorative approach. The peaceable schools movement, popularized by educators Bodine, Crawford, and Schrumpf, developed programs for schools that teach conflict resolution education through individual applications (such as anger-management instruction), through classrooms (such as negotiation instruction integrated into curriculum designs), through school-side programs or policies (such as a checklist of restorative policies), and through community programs (such as Big Brothers/Sisters).[9]

This approach seeks to create a culture of nonviolence by creating peaceful climates and by teaching negotiation and mediation skills to students. Restorative discipline embraces the peaceable schools approach, yet focuses more intentionally on restorative practices that can be used when harm is done.

Both arms of restorative discipline—the preventive and the restorative—acknowledge the value of conflict in the learning process. Educational psychologists Johnson and Johnson report that learning usually, if not always, requires conflict.[10] And, as Piaget and others have said, conflict pro-

---

vides the dissonance that energizes the assimilation and accommodation processes of learning.

Discipline from a restorative perspective may be compared to a checking account. If you take money out and make no deposits, you become bankrupt. When a child is disciplined, a withdrawal is made on the *relationship* account. The relationship account itself is based on respect, mutual accountability, and even friendship established within a caring community. If the substrata work of community-building has not been done, the child is bankrupt and has nothing to lose by misbehaving or by being confronted. The child's motivation to change is limited.

Educators commonly speak of a 5:1 ratio (deposits: withdrawals) in order for students to achieve academically. Whenever a child is confronted for misbehavior, the relationship experiences withdrawal or strain. Accordingly, a teacher would need to provide five affirmations for each confrontation. Both the affirmative/instructional and the restorative arms are needed for learning and for motivation to occur in classrooms.

Nelsen, Lott, and Glenn say, "Research has shown that the greatest predictor of academic success is the students' perception of 'Does the teacher like me?'"[11] Unless children feel cared for, they may not feel safe enough to risk performing academically or care enough to resist draining life from the community. However, if meaningful relationships are already established before things go wrong, people are more likely to be motivated to work out their differences through conversation than if these relationships are absent. My own (Judy's) research shows that this is also true among children with learning disabilities.

However, even though relationship-building may work to create academic success, it is not the only reason we try to cultivate good relationships in schools. It is simply the right thing to do as caring human beings. The peaceable schools movement seeks to create and nurture relationships. The restorative arm seeks to mend relationships when they are damaged or broken.

A peaceable school is defined by its practices, those day-to-day actions that build positive relationships and caring communities. Brennan Manning notes that there are no neutral actions: in every moment we either drain life or give it.[12] Therefore, the choices children make are either life-draining or life-enhancing actions. In order to develop the self-discipline to choose well, students must understand the effects of their actions on others, as well as the many choices of behavior available to them.

> There are no neutral actions— we either drain or give life.

Restorative discipline provides a framework to support learning communities by modeling and encouraging responsible behavior and discouraging harmful behavior. Schools that view conflict as a teachable moment and an opportunity for growth intentionally design environments and processes that value relationship-building and community-building. The process begins with examining the models used not only for children but for adults: the teachers, administrators, and staff persons. If children do not see these processes practiced among adults and within the procedures they experience, they will not believe in the value of transforming conflict.

Characteristics of peaceable schools

The following are some indicators or characteristics of schools that provide a peaceable or restorative environment. (Unless otherwise indicated, the personal illustrations come from Judy.)

1. Educators as models of restorative practices: What are you modeling in your school?

The kind of person you are affects whether students want to change or even know how to change. We know what is possible by observing what we see around us. Conflict Resolution Education for teachers should precede CRE for students. Do educators teach from a caring framework? Do educators and staff see their mission as the development of the whole child, not just the child's academic self?

Are the values of care, respect, and sensitivity honored in the hiring process? Is restorative justice honored in polices and practices in adult-to-adult relationships within the school? Does the professional development program include instruction in restorative practices?

Restorative justice guidelines (pages 25-26) can be listed in checklist form and then used as a meter stick for assessing the school's restorative justice efforts. Because students readily sense hypocrisy, this meter stick should be used to assess faculty-staff-administration policies and practices before implementing them with students. When students see adults treat each other with care, they are more likely both to model the behaviors and to actively engage the restorative practices offered to them.

2. A physical ethos of care in the classroom: What does the environment look like, sound like, and feel like?

Are there safe spaces and places for collaborative and restorative work? Are differences honored? What boundaries are evident in student conversations? Is the space inviting for visitors and regular attendees? What is already in place that invites collaboration and restoration? The language we use to describe components of schools also influence the social context. For example, schools that rename their lunchrooms as "dining rooms" often report greater respect and civility than when "cafeteria" is the common descriptor.

One private high school in Virginia attaches small white boards with markers to the outside locker doors of students. Students can send notes to each other via the boards, and students relish the opportunity to wish someone a happy birthday, or to write words or symbols of encouragement before school events and exams. The handbook views this communication option as a privilege, and writers are accountable for choosing words that honor the school's philosophy and mission. Every year I take an Ethos Walk[13] through this school with local teachers, and they never fail to note the atmosphere of care they themselves feel after reading the locker comments.

> View punishment as a step toward more life-giving behavior choices.

3. An emotional ethos of care in the classroom: What are the routines, procedures, and practices in classrooms?

What plan is in place to give students control of routines and rules, use of time, and friendly class rituals: beginnings and endings, transitions, community-building activities, cooperative learning, and community meetings? How is conflict in the classroom handled? Is there a developmental discipline model in place that views punishment as a transition to more life-giving behavior choices? Does the plan include movement from consequences to solutions to restoration?

Some classrooms establish peace tables or negotiation corners where students go to solve their problems with each other. One high school music teacher in Indiana "circles up" his choir on days when something seems to be interfering with their performance. He asks them to share what barriers they're experiencing and then brainstorms about ways to meet both individual needs and to maintain focus on growing as a choir. By consensus, they choose actions to achieve those goals. The process becomes one more strategy for encouraging community ownership and accountability.

4. Restorative school structures: What are the mission, policies, and practices of the school community?

Is the identity and purpose of the school demonstrated in the moment-to-moment happenings of school life? Teachers need mediation and negotiation training, too, and they need to use it among themselves. Do administrators view teachers as a means to an end or an end in themselves? Is there curriculum mapping for emotional literacy?

> Teachers need mediation and negotiation training, too.

My middle-school daughter once asked if she could quit a community choir she belonged to for three years. When I asked why, she said, "The director seems to care more about my voice than about me. I don't like that. It's not fun to sing anymore." No one likes to feel used. When the perceived focus becomes the content over the person, people feel used. When teachers are valued only for the test scores of their students, they feel used. When administrators are "successful" only when they achieve "highly effective school" status, they feel used. Eventually, "used" people lose joy in learning and teaching.

Curriculum does not teach; teachers do. Standards don't encourage; administrators do. Peaceable schools value personnel and students for who they are as worthy human beings. The president of a liberal arts college in Kansas notes that the success of his college rides on faculty and staff who engage each student as uniquely gifted. Faculty regularly spend hours advising and encouraging students regarding their life choices, even when students will not be continuing at the college. If your mission statement says you care, then specific practices of care should be habits within your school.

5. Conflict Resolution Education (CRE): How is conflict resolution taught in schools?

How do students learn the skills of negotiation, mediation, and consensus-building? Do they learn strategies to address conflict while studying history, literacy, math, PE, and science? Is there a curriculum that connects conflict-resolution development across disciplines, a curriculum of identity that helps students discover their interpersonal gifts, and a curriculum of exercise that encourages students to practice habits of goodness?

Educators of K-12 children can find numerous published curriculums for these skills which can be adapted to their specific subjects.[14] Suggestions are presented in the Selected Resources on page 84 of this book.

Teachers sometimes incorporate the guidelines for resolving conflict into their classroom rules or covenants of conduct. For example, these common negotiation rules—agree to talk it out, listen without interrupting, and use polite language—can be articulated under the general classroom or school rule to "Respect Others."

6. *Kindness curriculum: How are habits of kindness directly taught in schools?*

Students need to be taught to identify their emotions and to manage them appropriately. They can learn to appreciate, affirm, and initiate caring behavior. They can also learn active listening and ways to accurately and politely express their needs in order to prevent problems and to creatively solve them.

Peace begins with being included and with including others. Getting along means respecting other perspectives, developing empathetic accuracy, and understanding prejudice and how it works. Kindness is learned by planning and implementing celebrations. Children learn to trust, help, and share with each other. These characteristics can be present and taught in classes.

> We learn empathy as we are asked to find it within ourselves.

I encountered a lunchtime problem in a classroom for elementary children receiving behavior support. I was the university supervisor for the student teacher, who explained to me that she needed to be on duty while I was there and could not meet to talk about her teaching. Without her vigilance, she said, Sean would probably attempt to steal the homemade cookies Jasper brings each day. Sean headed to the restroom, and I asked the student teacher if I could speak to Jasper.

"What do you think will happen if you put one of those awesome cookies on Sean's desk before he comes back?"

"I think he'd just eat it."

"I think he'll do something else first; he will look surprised, and then he'll smile and look up at you. How could we find out?"

"I could put a cookie on his desk real quick." He burst from his chair and placed the cookie in the middle of Sean's desk.

"Where will we sit so we can see his response?"

We each chose a different angle to view Sean's return. Sean did not notice the cookie until he sat down, and then a big smile lighted his face. He looked at Jasper. He said nothing; he simply looked at Jasper. The student teacher told me on my next visit that Jasper has eaten with Sean every day since that event.

We learn empathy as we are asked to find it within ourselves. Empathy often fosters compassion and motivates right choices. When we ask children to put themselves in another's shoes, possibilities can become reality.

7. From differentiated instruction to differentiated discipline: How is discipline differentiated in various school contexts?

If we believe that instruction should be matched to individual strengths, then should we not choose different discipline strategies for different students? Understanding the emotional intelligence and needs of children helps educators and students select processes that maximize student strengths and empower them to change.

Someone stole Allison's gym shorts as she showered after PE class. Allison was told that she would not be admitted to her seventh grade PE class unless she bought new regulation shorts from the PE department. The next day she took to school the $10 necessary to buy the shorts and put the money in her locker before attending class. As Allison returned to her locker she noticed a young man, someone who rode on her bus, slamming her locker door and rushing away. A student nearby told Allison that the fleeing student had kicked open her locker and had taken something from it.

Allison's explanation to her gym teacher didn't get her into the gym that day, and when she approached her homeroom teacher with the story she was told, "Allison, you're not supposed to bring money to school." With urging from her parents, Allison approached her principal and was told again, "I'm sorry, Allison, but the rule is 'No money in school.'"

When I shared this story with middle-school parents, I heard new stories around the same theme: the rule that's easiest to enforce is the one that's enforced. That often leads to a victim being ignored or a victim being blamed.

When we rely on rules rather than on relationships to guide our responses to harm, everyone loses. Families view the school as uncaring and may contribute less to the school. Victims feel helpless and abused and may invest less in their schoolwork. Bystanders are less likely to say what they saw because nothing changes in the end. Educators and administrators are frustrated because they feel they only have limited options. Wrongdoers blame their victims, and when someone eventually holds them accountable, they don't understand their responsibility or the need to be accountable.

> When we rely on rules rather than relationships when harms' been done, we all lose.

For example, the situation described above might embolden a young man to steal again. If he steals an unlocked car and gets caught, he might think, "Why should I be punished when the owner is responsible for not locking the car? The owner's just asking for it." One incident can contribute to a downward spiral in community relationships.

What if restorative conversations honoring the unique needs of those harmed and those who harmed could have taken place in this situation? Instead of levying predetermined consequences—or even none at all—what if a conference was convened involving those affected? The viewers, bystanders, victims, and significant adults in the life of those harmed and those who harmed would gather to decide what would make things right and prevent similar behaviors in the future.

Flexible policies

Many schools are already implementing restorative approaches through their policies, even though they may not be using that terminology. Lorraine provides the following example of a school whose disciplinary policies are not necessarily restorative, but they have enough flexibility to allow a restorative response.

This school has a specific "substance use policy for co-curricular activities" that applies to any student involved in a co-curricular activity, leadership position, public performance, or other activity related to school or under the supervision of school personnel. The policy is in effect 24 hours a day, 365 days a year while a student is enrolled at this private school.

If an offense occurs during the school year, the student will be suspended from extra-curricular activities for a period of 40-60 calendar days from the date of the offense. However, this school also has a policy that includes "the right to take additional disciplinary action, and to apply more or less severe penalties than the ones described in these guidelines, in its discretion." That latter policy provided the flexibility to use a restorative approach in this incident.

Ten students at the school who were either members of the basketball team or student council were found to have violated the school policy by drinking during a weekend party at one student's house. After much deliberation, energy, and time-consuming preparation, the school decided to work out a "restorative covenant" with each student that could reduce suspension time. Some of those activities included, but were not limited to, participation in a restorative justice circle (see next chapter), community service, mentoring, physical labor, and other educational activities.

Several months after the offense, 35 students, parents, and faculty came together for a restorative conferencing circle to respond to questions such as these:

- What did you think or feel when you found out that parents, administrators, and friends learned that you had been drinking that night? (Students respond.)

- How have things been for you between then and now? (All participants respond.)

- Who do you think has been affected by your actions and how? (Students respond.)

- What were you thinking or feeling at the time you found out about the drinking? (Parents, teachers, and administrators respond.)

- How have things been for you between then and now? (All participants respond.)

- Are there additional things that need to happen to restore you to the community and rebuild the community's trust? (Students respond.)

- Are there additional things you would like to add? (Parents, teachers, and administrators respond.)

The three-hour circle gave students, parents, administrators, and teachers a time to talk more about their hopes and fears as a result of what happened. It also provided an opportunity to share openly and honestly about what it would mean to reintegrate these students into their school and community life. Many saw this

We learn empathy as we are asked to find it within ourselves.

time of conversation as a gift and wished it had happened sooner in the process. Others recognized that more work was needed for trust to be restored.

All of this was possible, however, because the school-board's policy allowed for something outside of the "guidelines." Schools obviously need to have policies that ensure the safety and respect of all its members. But the policies can allow for other creative options that are life-giving and forward-looking, as the above school has shown. The following chapter explores some of these options.

5.
Models and Applications of Restorative Discipline

In the preceding chapters we discussed principles and values of restorative justice and the importance of creating an overall peaceable and restorative school environment. In this chapter we describe some specific models and applications of restorative discipline in schools. We acknowledge that it is sometimes difficult to separate the model from the application, and we have tried whenever possible to give examples of the models we discuss.

Whole-school training approaches

Conversation Peace, a restorative initiative in secondary schools, was developed as a collaborative effort of the Fraser Region Community Justice Initiatives Association and the Langley School District #35 in Langley, British Columbia. They offer trainings within the school district for teachers and students on four 6½-hour days. First, they teach Restorative Action philosophy, as well as communication skills, and then proceed with mediation training.[15]

Recognizing the importance of developing comprehensive programs within schools, the Colorado Schools Mediation Program has implemented a whole-school approach that focuses on training. Areas of training include anger management, bullying prevention and intervention, conflict resolution, curriculum integration, diversity and awareness issues, peaceable classrooms, peer mediation, positive discipline, and restorative justice mediation training.[16]

Reintegration following suspensions

Suspension from school or classrooms is a common disciplinary action in many schools, often associated with "zero tolerance" policies. The Center for the Prevention of School Violence in Raleigh, North Carolina, gives the following facts about school suspensions:

• Higher rates of out-of-school suspension are associated with lower rates of achievement in reading, math, and writing.

• States with higher rates of out-of-school suspension also have higher overall rates of juvenile incarceration.

• Racial disparity in out-of-school suspension is associated with similar disparity in juvenile incarceration.[17]

Many parents, youth advocates, and education experts are alarmed at the toll zero tolerance policies are taking. Research shows that suspension and get-tough policies are not making our schools safer nor our children behave. Excluding our children from school seems to be a precursor to them entering the legal system as they face academic failure, which often, in turn, leads to higher school dropout rates. Some have called it the "school-to-prison pipeline."

Although school suspensions may not be entirely eliminated, some schools are working to ensure that students stay connected through on-going educational opportunities, even though they may not be in their traditional classroom setting. Later in this chapter we will look at some of the ways restorative processes are being used to reduce the use of suspensions.

When suspensions happen, however, many are recognizing that a plan is needed to reintegrate those students into their classroom or school once they do come back. In the St. Joseph, Missouri Schools, a project supported by funding from the Juvenile Justice and Delinquency Prevention Challenge Grant Program was implemented during the 2001-2002 school year through Missouri Western State College.[18] The grant provided funding to add a restorative justice facilitator to an existing in-district suspension program for middle school students. The facilitator trained the students in restorative justice concepts during their 10-day stay in suspension, referred to as the Recovery Room. When students re-entered their school, a restorative justice circle process was held which included the student, parent(s), a school administrator, the guidance counselor, and teachers, as well as other students who may have been harmed.

> Research shows that suspensions are not making schools safer.

Program implementation included training in restorative justice, not only with students in the program, but with school and district administrators and teachers also. When a circle was held, letters were sent to parents informing them of the program and requesting their participation in a restorative justice circle before their son or daughter would be reintegrated into the school setting.

All participants of the circle met with the facilitator before the date of the circle to ensure their voluntary participation and agreement that basic circle guidelines would be followed. Guidance counselors followed up with students who participated in the circle to ensure that any agreement was being completed.

The students involved in this project during its first year were from four different middle schools and were in either seventh or eighth grades. A total of 76 students were referred to the district suspension program and 40 participated in a restorative justice circle. Of those 40 who returned to the suspending school, the number of students referred to the office decreased as noted below:

Reason for office referral	Before the Recovery Room	After the Recovery Room
Refusal to work in class	17 (55%)	7 (23%)
Incomplete assignments	9 (29%)	2 (6%)
Fighting	3 (10%)	1 (3%)
Disrespect to staff	22 (71%)	8 (26%)
Cussing	7 (23%)	2 (6%)
Stealing	2 (6%)	0 (0%)

Average number of unexcused absences prior to the Recovery Room: 2.2

Average number of unexcused absences after the Recovery Room: .23

In follow-up surveys, vice principals participating in the circles made the following comments when asked about favorable aspects of the circle process:

- "We had closure on the incident which had led to Recovery Room suspension."

- "Students took ownership, plans were made for success, and all parties knew the plan."

- "It became a chance to meet parents."

- "This was an opportunity for students to make amends with teachers and fellow-students."

- "It allowed students to know how others had been affected."

These administrators were also hopeful that restorative justice could be used in other ways at their schools. Students were asked about why they chose a restorative justice circle process. They responded:

- "So I could apologize to my teachers."

- "Because it helped me repair the harm."

- "To make sure the teachers really understood I was sorry and to make sure they know I'm really trying."

- "Because I knew what I did was wrong, and to apologize."

- "I chose a restorative justice conference because I didn't want to be thought of as a person who never apologized."

The St. Joseph, Missouri project demonstrated that restorative justice can be a promising approach for reintegrating students who have been suspended. Ideally, however, the *need* to suspend students can be reduced as well. The following models are being used by some schools to create problem-solving and disciplinary processes that minimize the use of suspension.

Class meetings
Recently Lorraine had a conversation with a fifth-grade student specifically about some of the classroom rules established at the beginning of the school year. His response

was, "I don't remember, but it doesn't matter anyway because our teacher never follows them."

She then asked, "Did your class help to come up with the rules?"

"Not really," he responded. "[The teacher] wrote them on the board and asked if we all agreed to them, but that was it."

Children have a need to belong to a group, to feel accepted, and to believe that their thoughts and opinions matter. Class meetings provide an opportunity to discuss issues and concerns important to them, rather than having activities that revolve only around the prescribed curriculum. If one of the goals of education is to teach our children vital skills for living, such as communication, learning to listen, and learning to participate meaningfully because their thoughts are valued, then the time required to conduct class meetings is a crucial investment in our children's lives.

Restorative approaches

- **reduce suspensions**
- **provide reintegration.**

In the book, *Positive Discipline in the Classroom*, Nelsen, Lott, and Glenn talk about the eight building blocks for effective class meetings:[19]

1. Form a circle.
2. Practice compliments and statements of appreciation.
3. Create an agenda.
4. Develop communication skills.
5. Emphasize learning about individual realities that might be different than the children's own.
6. Help them recognize the reasons people do what they do.
7. Practice role-playing and brainstorming.
8. Focus on non-punitive solutions.

These building blocks can be used to create an atmosphere where every person feels his or her voice matters, where students are allowed to learn according to their needs, and where life skills are taught and valued. It provides an opportunity to find new ways to successfully resolve issues and conflicts that inevitably arise as students and teacher become a classroom community. The circle processes described below provide an excellent way to create this atmosphere.

Circles

Circle processes are becoming increasingly popular in the restorative justice field. They are being used not only in cases of wrongdoing but also as a way to dialogue on difficult issues and for community problem-solving. These circle processes, which first entered the field from indigenous communities, provide for an inclusive process that includes not only those who are in conflict or were involved in the harm, but other members from the relevant community as well.

Circles provide an orderly and reflective process that reinforces positive values.

Various types of circles are used in the field, with a variety of names: peacemaking circles, healing circles, talking circles, etc.[20] Briefly, for any circle process, chairs are placed in a physical circle. One or two facilitators, often called keepers, lead the meeting. A talking piece is passed, usually clockwise, and only the person holding the talking piece is authorized to speak. People may pass the talking piece without speaking if they wish, and only one person speaks at a time.

After introductory comments, often including a discussion of values underlying the process, the keeper poses a question or a topic, then passes the talking piece. Circles usually involve a number of rounds. Since only one person speaks at a time, and participants have a chance to reflect on others' words and what they themselves will say, circles provide an orderly and reflective process that reinforces the underlying values of restorative discipline and peaceable schools. Some key elements of circle processes are summarized below:

Key elements of circle processes

Use of circles are based on the premise that

- each of us wants to be connected to others in a good way.

- each of us is a valued member of the community and has a right to his or her beliefs.

- we all share some core values that indicate what connecting in a good way means (even though being connected in a good way and acting from our values are not always easy to do, especially during times of difficult conversations or conflict).

Circle keepers

- do not control the circle but help participants uphold its integrity.

- help to hold a space that is clear, open, respectful, and free. This means knowing when/how to interrupt, when to open and close the circle, when to take a break, and how to remind people to adhere to the agreed-upon guidelines.

- are participants in the circle, not observers.

- don't need to be a mediator or group facilitator in the usual sense; it's not a position of power, but it is a responsibility to others to keep to the values of the circle.

A talking piece

- is an object of focus accepted and used by the group. Often something is used that has special meaning to the group.

- provides greater opportunity for listening and reflection since a person has to wait for the talking piece to come around before speaking. Participants tend to focus more on what people are saying than on preparing an immediate response.

- prevents one-on-one debates since people cannot respond out of turn.

- encourages shared responsibility for discussion.

- reinforces equality in the circle since it provides equal opportunity for all to participate.

- provides more opportunity for those who are often silent to be heard since they don't have to compete with those who are more verbal.

Guidelines when using the talking piece:

- Be respectful even though you may not always agree.

- Speak only when you have the talking piece.

- Be honest and speak only for yourself.

- Speak briefly so everyone who wants to has an opportunity to speak.

- You can pass the talking piece without speaking if you choose.

- Respect confidentiality as decided upon by the group—what's shared in the circle stays in the circle.

- There are no right or wrong answers in the circle.

Circle processes may be used in many ways. In Boston, for example, they are being used to reduce tensions and gang violence in the inner city.[21] Circles that include gang and community leaders, as well as police and city authorities, have allowed people to begin to understand each other and have reduced levels of violence. In Barron County, Wisconsin, elementary school teachers are using circle processes within the classroom for various class meetings.[22] Following are some of the applications for their circles:

Beginning-of-day circles

Circles at the beginning of each day can help develop common understandings of guidelines, expectations, and values. They can also be used to address tensions or problems that may have arisen the day before. A daily circle process provides a chance to check in with questions or issues such as:

- How was your night?

- What's going on in your life right now?

- What are your thoughts or reflections on today's assignment?

- Clearing details and expectations of daily schedules.

Anytime circles:

Circles can be used at any point when tensions or problems have arisen, or when decisions need to be made. They provide a problem-solving forum that teaches values such as honesty, accountability, responsibility, and compassion. Possible uses include:

- Dealing with behavior issues such as teasing, stealing, fighting, threats, playground problems.

- Sharing: show-and-tell, a birthday present.

- Brainstorming: creative writing ideas, how to spend class money, class projects.

- Discussing: news articles, current events, books, controversial topics.

- Having fun or doing a cooperative activity such as telling jokes and story-telling.

- Engaging in student-chosen discussion topics.

End-of-day circles

Circles are often used at the end of the day for purposes such as these:

- To share something that happened to each participant that day.

- To address a problem or conflict that has arisen during the day.

- To address feelings and tensions that may have developed inside the classroom, in other areas of the school, or even in the outside world (e.g., disturbing events in the news).

- To debrief the day (perhaps with each participant using one or two words to summarize the day).

Circles can also be used at all educational levels to deal with incidents between friends (or former friends), issues between a teacher and students, and so on. Below is an example of a farewell circle used in an Alternative Learning Center in Harrisonburg, Virginia.

Farewell circles and rituals

Farewell circles have become part of the cultural landscape in a university/public-school partnership alternative education program, designed to serve a handful of eighth graders who struggle with the social and cultural aspects of formal schooling in Virginia. Students are tutored and mentored by college students and a director who infuse restorative justice measures into the community education process.

> Circles can be used when tensions develop.

When a student leaves the program, and at the end of each semester when some tutors end their work, farewell circles mark their time together and encourage reflection and hope about each other's futures. Strategies used within the circle are chosen by students or educators to meet the individual needs of participants. Some of these rituals are repeated several times during the year.

A favorite ritual is the planting of seeds. A cake pan with dirt, a bowl of water, and a bowl of grass seed are placed in the center of the table. Each person is encouraged to sow and water a few seeds, and then share what seeds have been planted within them through the relationships being honored that day; e.g., "You stretched me to do something I wouldn't have done otherwise." Future intentions are honored as they also describe what they hope will continue to grow in them in their new job or placement or in the next semester.

These rituals are accompanied by written farewells, and each participant gives a question to be pondered to the person leaving. A group picture or collage of pictures is also presented to the one who is leaving. Sometimes a rose and a thorn are passed around the group, with each participant sharing a memory of a "thorn" or tough time that yielded important growth, and a "rose" or a story of a good time shared together.

The director once led an activity using grapes in one bowl and salty water in another bowl. Students and tutors dipped their fingers into the salty water, a symbol of tears shed as they worked in community, and then selected a grape to eat, symbolizing the sweetness of life. As they sampled the symbols, they identified times of tears and times of sweetness shared during their time together.

> We remember first and last things best.

The first time this ritual was offered, students seemed resistant, and some chose not to reveal a "salty" story. Later in the semester they explained their reticence: men don't cry. The ensuing conversation explored this stereotype, and at the end of the semester a male student asked to repeat the ritual.

Every farewell ends with food, an informal opportunity to express something beyond the usual give-and-take. Psychologists tell us that we remember first and last things best. We sow seeds for future community when we send away with joy and special remembrances those who have touched our lives.

School staff circles

Nancy Riestenberg, prevention specialist for the Minnesota Department of Education, talks about the use of circles by school administrators to organize staff meetings, to address staff conflicts, and to focus staff before the school day starts.[23] Given some of the difficulties schools have faced in recent years, circles have been used to work at staff mental health needs and to address what Riestenberg calls "compassion fatigue."

Recovery school circles

At the PEASE Academy in Minnesota, a high school serving teenagers who are recovering from chemical addiction, circles have become a way to work at the many struggles within the school community. Angela Wilcox, a teacher at the Academy says:

> When a student needed to leave the community due to an incident of using [drugs], there was no good way to communicate this to the rest of the student body without violating the student's confidentiality . . . The circle changed all of that. Every student who makes choices that lead to being asked to leave the school, whether for a relapse, for breaking probation for academics or attendance, or for behavior reasons, is given the choice of doing a circle with the rest of the school. In the circle, the student can address the issue, make amends if necessary, and ask for support and feedback. By using a circle to process these issues, everyone knows what has happened and why the student is leaving, as they hear it directly from the source and can express their grief, anger, or support. Circles like this essentially eliminate gossip.[24]

Conferencing

When serious harms are committed, restorative discipline provides an opportunity for those harmed and those doing the harming to talk together. Conferencing allows them to share what happened, how each feels about it, what needs to be done to make the matter right, and how to avoid this situation in the future.

Conferencing provides a forum to explore:

- what happened,

- how participants felt about it,

- what needs to be done to make things right,

- and how the situation might be prevented in the future.

Sometimes a circle process is appropriate, involving a range of participants. Other times the process may look more like a "family group conference" or community group conference as used in New Zealand and elsewhere.[25] This latter process involves some authority figures and is empowered to decide on the full range of sanctions and outcomes. Often, though, the process will be much a like victim/offender conference or mediation, with participants limited to those harming and those harmed, and perhaps a few family members of both.[26]

In any of these processes, it is essential that the conference be facilitated by someone specifically trained for that procedure. Trained facilitators understand the specific issues of victimization and offender behavior, can properly assess the appropriateness of bringing participants together, and can provide a safe environment. It is also important that the facilitator is seen as impartial. Victim/offender conferencing and mediation have developed specific training and processes for its facilitators.

Victim/offender conferencing is a restorative justice practice used around the world. Over 500 programs operate in the United States alone, primarily in the criminal justice area. Cases are generally referred through the legal system to a specific victim/offender program within the community. Each case is screened for appropriateness, and prospective participants are met with separately to determine their interest and whether they are available for a joint meeting.

The following case illustrates a community conference within a school setting.

Mr. Stewart was a retired salesman who decided to drive bus for his local school district. It was a job he enjoyed for the past three years and one that allowed him to purchase a brand new pick-up truck debt-free. One month after purchasing his pick-up he came back to the school after his last run and discovered both sides of his truck had been scratched end-to-end. He immediately went to the school office to talk with Mr. Connor, the assistant principal.

Mr. Connor, in the meantime, knew that whoever scratched the pick-up likely belonged to one of the athletic teams since they were the only students allowed to walk through that particular parking lot, which was fenced in and led to the athletic fields. He brought in both the girls field-hockey team and the boys track team, the only two groups using the fields that day. Three names repeatedly came up as suspicious, but all three of those boys denied any knowledge of the incident. After several weeks of questioning and interview-

---

ing the three boys repeatedly, one finally admitted that the three of them scratched the truck with their cleats.

Two months after the incident, Mr. Stewart received a phone call saying that three boys had been identified as the ones doing the damage. He was asked whether he would like to meet with them to talk about what happened. A facilitator met with Mr. and Mrs. Stewart and heard their painful story about living in fear that this incident was somehow related to a disciplinary action Mr. Stewart had taken against a disruptive student on his bus months earlier. They feared for their safety, not knowing if this student would come to their house and cause further harm to them or their belongings.

While Mr. Stewart was relieved to learn that he did not know the boys who caused the damage, he wondered whether they were "put up to it" by someone else. He had many questions and was anxious to meet the boys, although Mrs. Stewart expressed her anxiety and declined to be present.

The three boys and their parents also met with the facilitator, acknowledging that they had no idea who owned the truck and that they realized that their actions were stupid and without cause. They agreed to a meeting with Mr. Stewart.

The meeting with Mr. Stewart, the three boys, their parents, the assistant principal, and the track coach took place at the school four months following the incident. Mr. Stewart expressed his anger and hurt about the damage the boys caused, the ensuing torment of not knowing why, and his fear that it was an act of revenge.

The boys told Mr. Stewart how it had happened, that it had been a stupid, impulsive act on their parts, and they expressed their regret for the pain they caused. The parents thanked Mr. Stewart for agreeing to meet with them, apologized for their sons' initial denial of involvement, and expressed concern for Mrs. Stewart's health related to this incident.

The track coach and assistant principal, while also expressing disappointment in the boys' initial denial, supported them in their decision to come forward, accept responsibility for their actions, and pay Mr. Stewart for the cost of repainting the entire truck. As the meeting ended, Mr. Stewart expressed his hope that he could drive the boys to a track meet so that he would get to watch them compete.

Truancy mediation

Truancy mediation as a process provides a relaxed atmosphere for the student, parents, and school personnel to discuss the truancy problem and come to some resolution. By utilizing the nonadversarial nature of mediation, all parties' concerns and views are heard, and a mutual agreement is likely to be reached to resolve the problem. In the 1998-99 school year, West Hills Middle School in West Jordan, Utah, and the Utah Administrative Office of the Courts, collaborated in an interagency pilot truancy mediation intervention program. The program was implemented to divert truancy cases from entering the juvenile court system.

This program has now been expanded to school districts throughout the state of Utah. In 2003, a total of 276 cases were mediated, and over 75 percent of the youth involved in these mediation sessions improved their school attendance and were not referred to the Juvenile Court. Of these 276 cases, 100 were part of a pilot program for elementary-age students. In this elementary-school pilot, only five youth and their parents were eventually referred to the Juvenile Court.[27]

In some ways, this Utah model looks more like a "community group conference" than traditional mediation. Participants include the student, the student's parents, and a team from the school (usually consisting of an assistant principal, a counselor, and the attendance secretary). The mediators in the program are trained community volunteers who are recruited, trained, and supervised by the Administrative Office of the Courts.

Truancy mediation improves communication between parents, schools, and students, and it provides a communication model based on respect and honesty, as together all parties search for a solution to make education a good experience. One of the most positive aspects is that students are active in the decision-making process, thus giving them more ownership in the solution and in carrying out the agreement.

One aspect of mediation often reported as a deterrent is the amount of time it takes out of the school day—usually 90-120 minutes. In the Utah program, the benefits are seen to have outweighed the cost in time. These include not having to take time to appear in court, the chance to build stronger community bonds, and the development of positive relationships between the school staff, the student, and the parents as they sit around the table together. The following is a case story from the school.

> Often parents, students, and school personnel are at odds when a case goes to mediation. This story from the Utah Administrative Office of the Courts shows the shifts that can occur during a mediation process.

A student had missed many days of school and was failing her classes. The school had made multiple phone calls and written letters to the mother about the absences and finally sent a referral to juvenile court for truancy. The school and the district were unacquainted with the Truancy Mediation program, but the probation officer and the judge hearing the case were informed and referred the case to mediation.

The mediator contacted the school, and staff agreed to participate. The attendance secretary explained that the school had tried to work with the mother to no avail. The mother and her husband had written accusatory and derogatory letters to the principal. School personnel believed that the mother was lying about her daughter's illness because someone from the school had seen her in town on days she had called in sick.

The mediator learned, through conversations with the mother, that she felt attacked by the school. She explained that her daughter really was ill on the days she was absent. She felt that the principal was uncooperative, hated her, and had judged her. She was angry and didn't feel like she could work with him.

During the mediation the girl began to cry when she was invited to talk about the attendance problem. She was afraid. The mediator helped her to understand that she was not in trouble and that everyone in the room wanted to help her find a solution to the problem. The attendance secretary also spoke up in a very reassuring way and told the girl and her mother that she was there to support them and help them work out a solution.

The school learned that the stepfather's job had taken him out of the country and that the mother felt quite alone and inadequate in dealing with this problem. The student missed her stepfather and was having trouble adjusting to her first year in middle school. She frequently had stomach pains. The mother didn't feel that she should force her daughter to attend when she was not feeling well. She didn't know what to do. Additionally, the mother didn't know how to access attendance and class information on the school's website.

The mother learned that there were people at the school who cared and could provide help, people who also had children and understood the importance of communication between parent(s) and the school.

As the mediation proceeded, a plan was developed for the mother to bring her daughter to school every day that she was not sick and to call the school in the case of any absences. However, if the student was having stomach pains, the mother would bring her to school and speak with school personnel about it. If necessary, the girl could be excused from her classes by the school counselor, who agreed to meet with the student on a regular and as-needed basis.

The school gave the mother information about accessing attendance and class information on the website and an application for their after-school club that provides help with homework and offers social activities.

The mother agreed to find outside help for her daughter if the school's interventions were not sufficient. The school was willing to provide a list of community resources. Together, the school, mother, and student created a written plan and requested that the court hold the case open for a review in 60 days. The judge agreed to this and planned to dismiss the case if the plan was followed.

> Five months later the attendance secretary reported that the student's attendance was no longer a problem. Connections had been established with the mother who now felt comfortable calling whenever she needed help. The bridge had been built.

Bullying

Bullying may be the most common type of violence in schools today. It is reported that almost 30 percent of U.S. teens are either a bully, a target of bullying, or both.[28] Most bullying incidents last less than a minute, with cyber bullying via instant messaging or mass emails occurring almost instantaneously. Bullying is defined as a pattern of intentional harm done over time, which can take physical, verbal, or proxemic forms. The last form translates into exclusion through social or personal distance, thus harming relationships.

In an article written by Brenda Morrison, she notes:

> Bullying at school causes enormous stress for many children and their families, and has long-term effects. School bullying has been identified as a risk factor associated with antisocial and criminal behavior. Bullies are more likely to drop out-of-school . . . victims are more likely to have higher levels of stress, anxiety, depression, and illness, and an increased tendency to suicide.[29]

She goes on to outline a framework, based on restorative justice principles, aimed at changing the bullying person's behavior, while keeping schools safe.

A 2003 report by Fight Crime: Invest in Kids states the epidemic proportions of bullying. "Of children in sixth through tenth grades, more than 3.2 million—nearly one in six—are victims of bullying each year, while 3.7 million bully other children."[30] The report lists three models that have been tested and proven as effective tools for bullying prevention:

- *The Olweus Bullying Prevention Program* was first developed by Dan Olweus in Norway. It brought about a 50 percent reduction in bullying in Norway, and a 20 percent reduction in bullying in a South Carolina test, which included 39 schools in six school districts.

- *Linking the Interests of Families and Teachers* (LIFT) has shown that long-term results are possible with a 10-week anti-aggression program.

- *The Incredible Years* was designed for children ages two to eight who have high levels of aggressive behavior. The program has been able to stop the cycle of aggression as it trains parents and children in problem-solving skills.

Restorative discipline engages a no-blame framework to support bully-free schools. An "education-for-and-by-community" approach focuses on the conditions which encourage respect and discourages bullying among all members of the community, not just among students. Teachers and administrators bully, too, and thus the hypocrisy of student-centered bullying prevention programs can discourage student involvement.

Peaceable schools discourage bullying by creating a caring ethos. Circle processes for educators, staff, and students promote fairness and build supportive relationships necessary for safe schools. Within regularly planned circles or morning meetings, persons engaged in the education of children become aware of bullying around them, share their experiences of bullying someone and being bullied, learn ways to communicate nonviolently, create guidelines for safe community, and support each other toward healthier ways of thinking and acting.

When bullying occurs, the goal becomes one of restoration and reintegration for all parties. Restorative community conferences or circles are sometimes held to engage all persons affected by the bullying. This is an occasion for all to hear the harm and to plan steps to accountability and reintegration. However, persons harmed by bullying or harassment may not wish to face the person who harmed them in a group setting, fearing further victimization. In these situations, a face-to-face meeting may not be advisable, and the one-to-one adult-to-student option described below may offer a more comfortable forum for restoration.

> Restorative discipline engages a no-blame framework to support bully-free schools.

One-on-one restorative processes with those affected by or involved in the bullying could include the following components:

- An initial, private meeting with the person harmed to hear his/her story, to create a safety plan, and to ascertain what he/she needs to put things right, organizing these items into an agreement, if appropriate.

- A private meeting with the wrongdoer to gather his/her perspective; to explore the motivations for the bullying; to explain the hurt that was caused; to encourage self-reflection, responsibility-taking, and new, more life-giving actions in the present and future; and to plan ways to put things right, using an agreement format if appropriate.

- A follow-up with both parties to assure that agreements have been met.

- An analysis of environmental variables that may have contributed to the incident. Do these incidents occur in certain contexts, within or between certain groups of students, in specific locations, or even during a particular time of day? What contextual or systemic variables foster, spark, or reward bullying behaviors? These findings should then be shared with an appropriate committee or group.

Questions and comments that support change for persons who have bullied might include:

- What did you do?

- What did you want to happen when you did that?

- Put yourself in (name of person harmed) shoes: how do you think he/she feels about what happened?

- Remember a time when someone hurt you. What happened? How did you feel?

- Everyone makes mistakes and hurts others. The important thing is to learn from one's mistakes. Do you want to be someone who fixes his/her mistakes? How can you make things better?

- What do you think (name of person harmed) needs in order to make things better? What else might be good to have happen?

- So, you've decided to address what happened by carrying out (name the agreements). How will you do that? When will you do it?

- Let's practice to find the best way. What will you do or say first?
- There may be a time in the future when you will feel like bullying. What will you do instead? Can you think of a time when you wanted to bully someone but decided not to? What were you thinking? Could you do the same in the future?

The Community Oriented Policing Services (COPS) in the Department of Justice advises in its report, "Bullying in Schools," that the "whole-school" approach advocated in the Olweus Bullying Prevention Program should be used.[31] Such an approach enlists the entire school by training *all* school staff, developing consistency in responses to bullying by all adults, and adopting school-wide anti-bullying rules. This holistic approach is more likely to be effective than programs that address bullying from only one or two directions.

> **A holistic approach is more likely to be effective than programs that address bullying from only one or two directions.**

This emphasis on whole-school approaches is critical to the philosophy of restorative discipline. Bullying prevention provides a good example of how a program, when implemented as a well-meaning stand-alone approach, can be counter-productive. The COPS report also provides advice against relying on such strategies as:

- "Peer mediation approaches. As Sue Limber of Clemson University warns, 'bullying involves harassment by powerful children of children with less power.'"[32]

Therefore, Limber argues, mediation approaches might even further victimize bullied children by assuming they have the power, without adult intervention, to prevent the bullying.

• Zero tolerance policies. The COPS report says that a zero tolerance approach "may result in a high level of suspensions without full comprehension of how behavior needs to and can be changed. It does not solve the problem of the bully, who typically spends more unsupervised time in the home or community if suspended or expelled.

• Simply advising victims to ignore or "stand up to" bullies. This can be unproductive or even dangerous without adequate adult support to prevent bullying in the schools.

These are but a few of the models and applications for applying restorative justice in a school setting. The possibilities are limited only by our imaginations.

6.
Ideas for Next Steps

Some schools have taken very seriously the idea of using restorative approaches. The following examples suggest some possibilities.

Whole-school approaches

In Barron County, Wisconsin, six area school districts have implemented a whole-school restorative approach. They are committed to restorative justice training for all administrators, teachers, and staff as a way of infusing restorative discipline practices in the classrooms, hallways, playground, and extra-curricular activities. The school districts have partnered with the Barron County Restorative Justice Program to bring practitioners into the school to trains others and conduct conferences or circles when school personnel are not available or cannot take time to prepare and facilitate.

As a side note, during a visit to Barron County, Lorraine was invited to participate in a circle in the middle school during a morning training-break with school teachers. The guidance counselor called the program director and asked if she would be willing to conduct a circle requested by six middle-school friends who were in conflict. We sat together for an hour, with the girls clearly understanding the function of the circle and happy to have a facilitator present to guide the questions and discussion.

Following the circle, which seemed to clearly satisfy the students, Lorraine asked them how they knew to request a circle. One girl responded, "Well, we know that sometimes we just need help working things out and this is the best way to do it." When pressed about how they knew about doing the circle, they said, "Oh, we've been doing this since third grade."

Following the initial training for school personnel in restorative justice philosophy, training is also provided for teachers in the various practices of restorative discipline, such as circles or conferencing. An additional training component is the "learning communities" program. This provides an opportunity for teachers to sign up to be part of small groups that meet together before or after school, during the lunch hour, or even over supper, to study and discuss some aspect of restorative discipline within their school setting. Teachers log the hours spent together and are compensated through a grant for the time spent deepening their understandings.

> "Misbehavior is primarily an offense against human relationships."

"After-school specials" or seminars also provide an opportunity for school districts to meet together to share their experiences and deepen their knowledge. The specials incorporate an educational as well as a collaborative component.

Finally, part of the implementation plan includes community suppers to inform and educate parents and the community. This is a time to provide information about the philosophy of restorative justice, to discuss the restorative approaches being implemented throughout the school district, and to enlist the support of local community members.

In Oshkosh, Wisconsin, the Oshkosh Area School District is in the first year of a two-year grant from the Wisconsin Department of Public Instruction which allows the district to introduce Restorative Justice Circle Conferencing into their schools. They are using circles to resolve issues of truancy, conflict, vandalism, and harassment, and are using them also as an alternative to traditional disciplinary measures.

The grant also provides opportunities for school staff to learn and implement restorative practices in their classes and in their schools through an initiative called Project Restore. Training will be conducted for school staff, students, and parents in pilot schools about the fundamentals of restorative justice as well as circle facilitation.[33]

Discipline that restores

Roxanne Claassen teaches eighth grade at Raisin City School in Raisin City, California. Together with her spouse, Ron Claassen, they have developed models of peacemaking that she uses in her classroom every day. They have written a curriculum, "Making Things Right," that Raisin City Elementary adopted about 10 years ago.[34] The principles in that document have led to a more peaceful school climate. In an article, "From Principles to Practice," Roxanne says:

> Some, if not most, of the problems students have with each other are not really problems caused by school but problems caused by relationship issues. Judy and Lisa had been good friends. When both of them became interested in the same boy, conflict developed. Judy did not see Lisa as a friend but as a threat to her relationship with Joshua. Lisa and Joshua were in the same class so they had a natural setting in which they were together. Even though Joshua was clearly interested in

Judy being his girlfriend, he also had a friendly relationship with his classmate Lisa.

When conflict developed, none of them had many strategies they could use to deal with it. Name-calling and "dogging" began at school. This eventually led to Lisa making harassing phone calls to Judy's house.

The school was unaware of any of this until Judy's mom came to talk to someone who she thought might be able to help with the problem. Luckily our school has a Discipline That Restores structure in place. Since I am the mediation coordinator, I was asked to get in touch with the girls and their mothers to arrange a meeting that would bring the problems out into the open so they could be discussed and resolved. This is an example of the first principle of Discipline That Restores, which states, "Misbehavior is viewed primarily as an offense against human relationships and secondarily as a violation of a school rule (since school rules are written to protect safety and fairness in human relationships)."[35]

Roxanne goes on to report that Raisin City Elementary students comprise 33-45 percent of honor-roll graduates in the district. While she's not sure what happens to students once they leave this deliberate restorative-discipline structure, she believes they take with them relational tools that will help them throughout their lives.

Restorative measures

In her article "Aides, Administrators, and All the Teachers You Can Get: A Restorative Training Guide for Schools," Nancy Riestenberg describes the implementation of restorative justice in school districts in Minnesota, which was initiated by concerns about zero tolerance policies that produced a significant rise in suspensions and expulsions.[36]

The largest grants were awarded to four districts for In-School Behavior Intervention and Restorative Schools Staff Training to implement and evaluate restorative policies over a three-year period (1998-2001). Restorative justice planners were hired to train administrators in Circle Processes to repair harm. Staff also were offered training in classroom management and/or Circle Processes, as well as student advocacy for social/emotional and academic problems.

Riestenberg reports three findings from the first round of grants and evaluation:

- Restorative practices, such as Circles to repair harm, are viable alternatives to suspension.

- Restorative philosophy and practices had classroom management and teaching applications.

- Staff hired on grant money inevitably leave a district when the grant money is spent.

Once grant money was spent, schools found it difficult to maintain restorative-justice planners in their budgets, resulting in inconsistent use of restorative practices. Therefore, a second round of grant money specifically for staff development was awarded to a range of applicants to increase the capacity of staff and administrators to use restorative practices as an integral part of their job. To date, more than 700 people have been trained, yielding significant developments and outcomes that continue to prove encouraging throughout the state.[37]

Research on positive youth development indicates that the learning environment is every bit as important as individual interventions for students' health outcomes. Building the capacity of the educators—aides, administrators, and teachers—to use problem-solving behavior management, restorative philosophies, and restorative practices provides students with much-needed support, while still holding them accountable to address the harms they have caused or experienced. Much is gained long-term by increasing the capacity of the staff already in place. If one adult can make a difference, imagine what can be done when all adults work together.

Citizenship in action

Belinda Hopkins, author of *Just Schools: A Whole School Approach to Restorative Justice,* describes initiatives in Great Britain that take the values and principles of restorative justice into schools.[38] She states that "in some instances the starting point for the school focus had been a concern that certain schools were becoming involved in victim-offender mediation and conferencing without appreciating the need for an environment conducive to restoration, rehabilitation, and re-integration."[39]

She is concerned that while these processes create opportunities for listening, for recognition of harm, and often for an apology, the broader community is often left out of the ongoing process of reparation. She concludes that a truly restorative approach, one that would put relationships at the center, has to work at both the reparative and preventive levels.

A challenge

At the beginning of this book we talked about community-building and its importance in learning and growth. We also know that living in community is hard work. It reminds us of Parker Palmer, who said this after living in community for a year: "Community is that place where the person you least want to live with always lives." After a second year in community he said this: "When that person moves away, someone else arises immediately to take his or her place."[40]

This is one component of being in community with others. There is also the view that Dewitt Jones talks about in his video, "Celebrate what's right with the world." He says,

"Start with what you do and do it better."

"I started out in life, as most of us do, holding the maxim that I won't believe it till I see it. Yet the more I worked for [National] Geographic, the more I realized I had it backwards; the way it really works is I won't see it till I believe it. That's really the way life works."[41]

It is important to acknowledge that we are all on a continuum in life with what we see and what we believe. It is the same with restorative justice approaches within schools. The idea of working on a total-school approach, one that includes awareness, education, structural changes, and ethos-building, may seem overwhelming to educators.

A place to begin may be to assess what restorative components are already being used. "Start with what you do and do it better" should be the mantra. Start with the belief that when we celebrate what's right, we will have the energy, creativity, and inspiration to work at changing what is wrong.

Endnotes

1. (Berkeley: University of California Press, 1984), p. 193.
2. Contributed by Connie Doyle of the Barron County Restorative Justice Program, Barron County, Wisconsin.
3. Contributed by Judy H. Mullet, one of the co-authors.
4. See Jane Nelsen, Lynn Lott, and H. Stephen Glenn, *Positive Discipline in the Classroom: Developing Mutual Respect, Cooperation, and Responsibility in Your Classrooms,* 3rd ed. (Roseville, CA: Prima Publishing, 2000), p. 120.
5. See Alfie Kohn, *Beyond Discipline: From Compliance to Community* (Alexandria, VA: Association for Supervision and Curriculum Development, 1996) and John J. Wheeler and David Dean Richey, *Behavior Management: Principles and Practices of Positive Behavior Supports* (Upper Saddle River, NJ: Pearson Education, Inc., 2004).
6. For more information on this New Zealand model, see Allan MacRae and Howard Zehr, *The Little Book of Family Group Conferences: New Zealand Style* (Intercourse, PA: Good Books, 2004).
7. (Intercourse, PA: Good Books, 2002).
8. In *Emotional Intelligence: Why It Matters More Than IQ* (New York: Bantam Books, 1995).
9. For a sample curriculum on teaching conflict resolution, see Richard J. Bodine, Donna K. Crawford, and Fred Schrumpf, *Creating the Peaceable School: A Comprehensive Program for Teaching Conflict Resolution* (Champagne, IL: Research Press, 1994).
10. See David W. Johnson and Roger T. Johnson, *Teaching Students to be Peacemakers* (Edina, MN: Interaction Book Co., 1995).
11. See *Positive Discipline in the Classroom,* p. 25.
12. In *Abba Child* (Colorado Springs: NavPress, 2002).
13. An Ethos Walk is a 30- to 60-minute tour of a school building in which teachers divide into groups, analyze a particular school area, and then describe affective aspects of the physical environment. Small groups focus on observing one or more of the following areas: classrooms; media center; art, music, and career development rooms; lounges; restrooms; gymnasium; locker

rooms; offices, dining room; hallways; landscaping or exterior of buildings; and athletic fields. These small groups record aspects of their assigned areas that "give life" and aspects that have "potential to give life" if strengths of the school are heightened.

14. For a curriculum map for K-12 schools which outlines a developmental sequence of knowledge and skills needed for consensus decision-making, mediation and negotiation, critical and creative thinking, communication, and emotion perception and orientation abilities, see Richard J. Bodine and Donna K. Crawford, *The Handbook of Conflict Resolution Education: A Guide to Building Quality Programs in Schools* (San Francisco: National Institute for Dispute Resolution and Jossey-Bass Publishers, 1998).

15. *Conversation Peace,* by Catherine Bargen et al., is available as a training manual and workbook for participants. It can be ordered through Langley School District #35, www.sd35.bc.ca or through Fraser Region Community Justice Initiatives Association at www.cjibc.org.

16. For more information on the programs, trainings, and resources available through the Colorado Schools Mediation Program, visit their website at www.csmp.org.

17. See www.ncdjjdp.org/cpsv.html.

18. See Katz and Gardner. All the results cited are presented in this study.

19. Second edition, p. 42.

20. For a fuller explanation of circle processes, see Kay Pranis, Barry Stuart, and Mark Wedge, *Peacemaking Circles: From Crime to Community* (St. Paul, MN: Living Justice Press, 2003), and Kay Pranis, *The Little Book of Circle Processes: A New/Old Approach to Peacemaking* (Intercourse, PA: Good Books, 2005).

21. See Carolyn Boyes Watson, "What Are the Implications of the Growing State Involvement in Restorative Justice?" in *Critical Issues in Restorative Justice,* eds. Howard Zehr and Barb Toews (Monsey, NY: Criminal Justice Press, 2004), pp. 215-226.

22. See www.bcrjp.org.

23. The Minnesota Department of Education has been involved in restorative justice work in schools for a number of years. Their helpful resource, Restorative Measures: *Respecting Everyone's Ability to Resolve Problems* is available online at http://education.state.mn.us/content/064280.pdf.

24. This excerpt is available from an article titled "PEASE Academy" by Angela Wilcox, a language arts and human rights teacher at PEASE Academy. It is available on the Minnesota Department of Education website listed above.

25. See MacRae and Zehr, *The Little Book of Family Group Conferences.* Real Justice has been training schools to use a somewhat different form of conferences. For more information, see www.realjustice.org.

26. These models are described briefly in Zehr, *The Little Book of Restorative Justice.*

27. Information and statistics provided to the authors via email correspondence from Kathy Elton, ADR Director, Utah Court Administrator's Office, 2005.

28. See "Facts for Teens: Bullying," from the National Youth Violence Prevention Resource Center, Rockville, MD at www.safeyouth.org.

29. See her 2002 paper, "Bullying and Victimisation in Schools: A Restorative Justice Approach," available at www.restorativejustice.org.

30. This report is available free of charge on the Fight Crime: Invest in Kids website. See www.fightcrime.org.

31. This report by Rana Sampson is available online at www.cops.usdoj.gov.

32. Ibid., pp. 23-24.

33. For additional information, visit the Oshkosh Area School District website at www.oshkosh.k12.wi.us.

34. This curriculum contains 32 activities to teach conflict resolution and mediation skills. Distributed by Center for Peacemaking and Conflict Studies, Fresno Pacific University, Fresno, CA. Additional information is available online at disciplinethatrestores.org.

35. In *Conciliation Quarterly* 19 (Spring 2000). Available from Mennonite Conciliation Services, MCC U.S., in Akron, PA. See www.mcc.org/us/peaceandjustice/mcs.

36. In VOMA Connections no. 13 (Winter 2003). This Victim Offender Mediation Association newsletter is available online at www.voma.org.

37. For further information about Minnesota schools' restorative initiatives, contact Nancy Riestenberg, a prevention special-

ist with the Minnesota Department of Education, by phone at 651.582.8433, or by email at nancy.riestenberg@state.mn.us.

38. (London: Jessica Kingsley Publishers, 2005).

39. See "Citizens in Action: Restorative Justice in Schools." Available online at www.transformingconflict.org.

40. See "Change Community, Conflict, and Ways of Knowing to Deepen our Educational Agenda." Available online at www.mcli.dist.maricopa.edu/fsd/afc99/articles/changel.html.

41. This video/training guide is available through Star Thrower Distribution Corp., St. Paul, MN, or at www.starthrower.com.

Selected Resources

Bodine, R.J. and D.K. Crawford. *The Handbook of Conflict Resolution Education: A Guide to Building Quality Programs in Schools* (San Francisco: Jossey-Bass Publishers, 1998).

Claassen, Ron and Roxanne Claassen. *Making Things Right* (Fresno, CA: Center for Peacemaking and Conflict Studies, 1998).

Comfort, R. "Evaluating Restorative Justice for Schools," *The Leader.* Retrieved January 12, 2004 from http://education.umn.edu/EdPA/licensure/leader/2004Spring/Justice.html.

Daltan, Joan and Marilyn Watson. *Among Friends: Classrooms Where Caring and Learning Prevail* (Oakland, CA: Developmental Studies Center, 1997).

Hopkins, Belinda. *Just Schools: A Whole School Approach to Restorative Justice* (London: Jessica Kingsley Publishers, 2004).

Jonas, Trisha S. and Randy Compton. *Kids Working It Out* (San Francisco: Jossey-Bass; The Association for Conflict Resolution, 2003).

Katz, Joanne J.D. and Carol Gardner. "Restorative Justice: Circle Group Conferencing in the St. Joseph, Missouri Schools, 2002" (St. Joseph, MO: Missouri Western State College, 2002).

Kriete, R. *The Morning Meeting Book* (Greenfield, MA: Northeast Foundation for Children, 2002).

Lipchitz, Lola. *Restorative Justice in School Settings.* Retrieved January 15, 2004 from http://www.iapeace.org/rj%20schools%20article.htm.

Mirsky, Laura. "SaferSanerSchools: Transforming School Culture with Restorative Practices." May 20, 2003. Available on-line: http://www.restorativepractices.org.

Selected Resources

North Carolina Department of Juvenile Justice and Delinquency Prevention—Center for Prevention of School Violence, 2003. www. cpsv.org.

O'Connell, Terry, Ben Wachtel, and Ted Wachtel. *Conferencing Handbook: The New Real Justice Training Manual* (Pipersville, PA: The Piper's Press, 1999).

Pranis, Kay. *The Little Book of Circle Processes: A New/Old Approach to Peacemaking* (Intercourse, PA: Good Books, 2005).

Statement of Restorative Justice Principles as Applied in a School Setting (London: The Restorative Justice Consortium, 2003). www. restorativejustice.org.uk.

Zehr, Howard. *The Little Book of Restorative Justice* (Intercourse, PA: Good Books, 2002).

About the Authors

Lorraine Stutzman Amstutz is Director of Mennonite Central Committee's (MCC) Office on Crime and Justice. In this capacity, she provides consulting and training for agencies and communities seeking to implement programs of restorative justice which specifically include a Victim Offender Mediation/Conferencing component. She has worked in the victim offender field since 1984.

Lorraine has co-authored the *Victim Offender Conferencing in PA's Juvenile Justice System* curriculum, as well as numerous articles. She has served on the international Victim Offender Mediation Association (VOMA) Board and currently serves on the Board of the local victim offender program in Lancaster County, PA.

Lorraine received her B.S. in Social Work from Eastern Mennonite University in Harrisonburg, VA (where she was awarded the Distinguished Service Award for 2002), and her Master's in Social Work from Marywood University, Scranton, PA.

Judy H. Mullet is a professor of education and psychology at Eastern Mennonite University, Harrisonburg, VA. Her doctoral studies included a dissertation on conflict resolution strategy choices of adolescents with learning disabilities.

Judy currently teaches undergraduate courses in psychology and graduate courses for teachers in education, peacebuilding, and restorative discipline. She conducts workshops on restorative measures for public and private agencies and has published work on alternative education in the *School Board Journal.* Judy has authored and co-authored two study guides accompanying the Rhythms of Peace video series for both public and private school audiences.

Judy received a B.A. from Eastern Mennonite University, and an M.Ed. in School Psychology from James Madison University, both in Harrisonburg, VA, and a Ph.D. from Kent (OH) State University.

METHOD OF PAYMENT

❒ Check or Money Order
*(payable to **Good Books** in U.S. funds)*

❒ Please charge my:
   ❒ MasterCard ❒ Visa
   ❒ Discover   ❒ American Express

\# _____

exp. date _____

Signature _____

Name _____

Address _____

City _____

State _____

Zip _____

Phone _____

Email _____

SHIP TO: (if different)

Name _____

Address _____

City _____

State _____

Zip _____

Mail order to: **Good Books**
P.O. Box 419 • Intercourse, PA 17534-0419
Call toll-free: 800/762-7171
Fax toll-free: 888/768-3433
Prices subject to change.

Group Discounts for

The Little Book of
Restorative Discipline for Schools
ORDER FORM

If you would like to order multiple copies of *The Little Book of Restorative Discipline for Schools* by Lorraine Stutzman Amstutz and Judy H. Mullet for groups you know or are a part of, use this form. (Discounts apply only for more than one copy.)

Photocopy this page as often as you like.

The following discounts apply:

1 copy	$4.95
2-5 copies	$4.45 each (a 10% discount)
6-10 copies	$4.20 each (a 15% discount)
11-20 copies	$3.96 each (a 20% discount)
21-99 copies	$3.45 each (a 30% discount)
100 or more	$2.97 each (a 40% discount)

Free shipping for U.S. orders of 100 or more!

Prices subject to change.

Quantity   **Price   Total**

_____ copies of **Restorative Discipline**   @ _____ _____

Shipping & Handling
(U.S. orders only: add 10%; $3.95 minimum) _____
For international orders, please call 800/762-7171, ext. 221

PA residents add 6% sales tax _____

TOTAL _____

800/762-7171 • www.GoodBooks.com